LITTLE BOOK OF
TRACTORS

LITTLE BOOK OF
TRACTORS

First published in the UK in 2012

© G2 Entertainment Limited 2013

www.G2ent.co.uk

Printed and bound in China

ISBN 978-1-907803-30-7

The views in this book are those of the author but they are general views only and readers are urged to consult the relevant and qualified specialist for individual advice in particular situations. G2 Entertainment Limited hereby exclude all liability to the extent permitted by law of any errors or omissions in this book and for any loss, damage or expense (whether direct or indirect) suffered by a third party relying on any information contained in this book.

All our best endeavours have been made to secure copyright clearance for every photograph used but in the event of any copyright owner being overlooked please go to www.G2ent.co.uk where you will find all relevant contact information.

Contents

The Origins Of Mechanised Farming

Farming is one of the oldest of human industries, and it is equally one of the most important. Along with the securing of shelter and water, the finding of food is one of the basic requirements for existence, and human ingenuity has given us agriculture to ensure that growing populations have been fed.

The earliest roots of farming can be traced back to around 10,000 years ago, to settlements in the Fertile Crescent stretching from Israel to Turkey. In one such settlement, at Catal Hüyük in present-day Turkey, there is evidence of people taking wild seeds from plants such as wheat, barley and legumes and using them for food – and also for planting for the following year. Before the development of agriculture, humans had lived by hunting animals, fishing and gathering plants from the wild.

Around this time, people started to settle down in fixed communities, and they began to domesticate animals: first cattle, then sheep, pigs and goats. These were the humble beginnings of the agricultural revolution.

Despite being invented at around the same time in several parts of the planet, it took many thousands of years for agriculture to spread to other areas of the world. It did not reach Britain until around 4000 BC, but in all that time farming methods barely changed and remained very primitive. At first, crude implements were fashioned out of tree branches or from animal jawbones, horns and antlers. Then, around 4000 BC, animals, particularly oxen and donkeys, were introduced to help pull ploughs.

It is during the rise of the great civilisations of the Egyptians, Greeks, Romans and Sumerians that we see the

THE ORIGINS OF MECHANISED FARMING

true beginnings of mechanised farming. On drawings on ancient clay tablets found in Mesopotamia – present-day Iraq, Turkey and Syria – we can see the use of a wheel depicted on farm carts drawn by oxen. Yet it took many hundreds of years before use of the wheel spread, owing to the fact that there were no roads as we know them today.

The domestication of oxen provided mankind with the pulling power necessary to develop the plough. The Romans continued to use the same methods of farming that they had used for centuries, but they did introduce the ard, a two-oxen plough, to Britain during their occupation.

This early form of plough consisted of a frame holding a vertical wooden stick that was dragged through the topsoil. This piece of equipment is still used in many parts of the world. The ard breaks up a strip of land directly along the ploughed path, which can then be planted. Fields are often cross-ploughed at right angles, and this tends to lead to squarish fields, often referred to as Celtic fields.

In Britain, from the Romans, through the Saxon era to the Middle Ages, the majority of people made their living by farming and raising herds of animals. Farming practices were still very crude and primitive by today's standards, however.

Throughout the Middle Ages, all manner and types of ploughs were built to till the land ready for the hand sowing of such seeds as emmer and einkorn wheat. Incidentally, early British law required every ploughman to make his own plough, and no one was entitled to use one unless they had constructed it himself.

The mechanisation of agriculture is considered to have truly begun with the invention of the seed drill by Jethro Tull in 1701. This piece of equipment, along with the Enclosures Acts of the 18th and 19th centuries, revolutionised farming.

Before the first Enclosures Act, around half of all Britain's farms were using the open-field system to grow crops, a system that had been used since the Middle Ages and had always provided sufficient food for the British population. Under this system, a typical village would have three or four fields around it – with each villager having thin strips of land in each field – and a piece of common land that anyone could use.

By 1770, landowners were forcing enclosures and enclosing the separate strips of land into one farm, so the land was henceforth held and farmed by individuals rather than by the community. As the 18th and 19th centuries progressed, and as more and more enclosures took place, the face of farming and the British countryside began to change, with fields getting larger and larger.

This encouraged land owners to experiment with new farming techniques. Farmers could now invest in new machinery for use on their land, work in one area and not waste time walking between strips of land.

By the middle of the 19th century, Britain's population had grown to around 22 million people. Industrial towns and factories had developed rapidly and industrial workers no longer had the time nor the space to grow their own food. They needed to be fed. Britain's agriculture was about to change; the tractor was about to be invented.

There are few inventions in history that have changed the landscape like the modern tractor. Nowadays it is perhaps the most recognisable vehicle in the countryside.

Steam Power

Experimentation with steam power began in the first century AD, when Hero of Alexandria developed the aeolipile, a primitive form of steam engine that consisted of a hollow sphere mounted below a water kettle. A fire beneath the kettle turned the water into steam, which travelled through pipes to the sphere. Two L-shaped tubes on opposite sides of the sphere allowed the gas to escape and in so doing gave a thrust to the sphere that caused it to spin.

The aeolipile was the first device known to have transformed steam into rotary motion. But although the machine was sophisticated, we need to move on to the early 17th century to find experimentation with real practical uses for steam.

Giambattista Della Porta succeeded in constructing a steam pump that was capable of raising water. His work was copied by the Frenchman Salomon de Caus, who is often erroneously credited as the inventor of the steam engine.

But the first commercially successful atmospheric steam engine was patented by the British inventor Captain Thomas Savery, who designed a machine with no pistons and no moving parts except for the taps for raising water. Savery took out a patent in 1698, calling his machine The Miner's Friend. His patent was adapted by Thomas Newcomen, who had much more success with his engine.

Both machines from Savery and Newcomen were used in the mining industry, but in the world of agriculture, the pace of development was growing. Steam traction engines became more refined and although they were originally built as small road locomotives and were generally used to provide power to drive equipment such as threshing machines, they did become a practical proposition for farm use.

Thomas Aveling, born in Ely, Cambridgeshire has become known as the father of traction engines. In 1856, he set up an agricultural repair business and produced a steam plough by modifying a Clayton and Shuttleworth portable engine,

LEFT
The boiler on an
old steam tractor

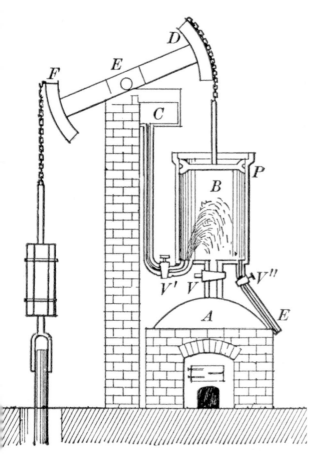

which had to be hauled from job to job by horses, into a self-propelled one by fitting a long driving chain between the crankshaft and the rear axle.

In 1861, Aveling started building steam engines to his own designs and then, wanting to expand, he joined forces with Richard Thomas Porter and formed the Aveling and Porter Company. Ultimately this company produced more machines than all the other British manufacturers combined.

Early traction engines, also known as steam tractors, are what we nowadays would refer to as showman's vehicles. But these early machines did pave the way for steam-powered machinery to be used on farms.

At first, farmers were sceptical about the new machinery. Although it could do the work of many men and horses, few farmers could afford to buy the equipment and many were concerned about the effect the weight of the heavy machines would have on the soil. In addition, it was often thought that to avoid the wheels of the new-fangled machine running over already ploughed ground, a team of horses would be needed to finish off the job anyway.

Steam Oddities

During the early days of tractor design, there were some very innovative inventions, most of which fell by the wayside and were never seen again. One of the most unique was the invention by the French army engineer Nicholas Cugnot who built a steam powered military tractor in 1769. This was the first machine designed for haulage although it could allegedly carry four people. It had three wheels, was capable of speeds of up to 4mph and had the impressive look of a kettle and the stability of a drunken person. The machine still exists and can be seen in the National Academy of Arts and Métiers in Paris where it has been since 1800.

Another odd design was James Boydell's steam tractor which he fitted with snow shoes. The idea was to enable the machine to operate on soft or snowy ground. Basically Boydell fitted a series of hinged boards around the rims of the tractor wheels. These acted in a similar way to skis and spread the weight of the machine. Boydell was Canadian but he successfully sold his idea to the British Army who used the machines in the Crimean War. Many of the machines were also exported to such far flung places as South America and Australia.

Oliver Evans was an American inventor, in fact he was a serial inventor and one of his madder ideas was the Orukuter Amphiboles. Put simply this was a steam amphibian tractor. Evans had been hired by the city of Philadelphia to build a dredger. Unfortunately his workshop was inland as well as miles from the dredging site. Evans's solution was to build an enormous combination that consisted of a car like structure together with a form of steam boat which he drove to the river that required dredging. There in 1804 it began its assigned work. The Orukuter Amphiboles was a complete failure as it was a mechanical disaster. It was broken up and sold and the world had to wait another hundred years for a true amphibious vehicle.

STEAM ODDITIES

The Pedestrian Roadside Digger is an apt name for one of Thomas Darby's inventions. Around 1879, he built a light traction engine that travelled broadside across fields on steam powered feet! The first version that was built had six feet and the second one had eight. This enabled it to walk over the fields. Unfortunately it had a tendency to jump and so wasn't a complete success. All the same it did get exported and there is evidence that one worked the prairies of Canada.

George Stockton Berry is credited with being the inventor of the world's first self-propelled combine harvester in 1886. At that time typical combines were being pulled by teams of horses or mules, so when the animals stopped so did the machinery. Berry came up with the idea of a combine propelled by a straw fired boiler. This meant that the farmers could use the waste straw to fuel the machine from the field as they worked. Unlike many previous machines, this one worked well and in 1888, equipped with a 40 foot header and using night-time lighting, one of Berry's combines cut over 100 acres in a twenty four hour period.

Orchard and vineyard tractors are a specialist type of tractor adapted with features to better suit the use in these areas. Around 1909, Alfred Johnson and his brother started to develop an orchard tractor in order to make it easier to farm the family orchards. They first put discarded iron horseshoes around the rim of the tractor wheels to help the machine work better on soft and uneven ground. This they sold to the Joshua Hendy Ironworks, a leader in the mining industry who in turn sold it to the M. & J. Rumely Company. The tractor seems to have been variously known as the Johnson Toe-Hold and Improved Johnson Tractor Model C.

Another interesting early tractor is the one designed by John Bean of farm sprayer fame. Bean's tractor had one crawler in the front and two steerable wheels in the back, one being the clutch and the other the steering wheel. With a 4 cylinder Le Roi engine, it had a turning circle of around 4 metres. Around 1,000 of these machines were built; many of them were sold to the Japanese at the end of WWI.

After Steam

By the end of the 19th century, road vehicles were being powered by the internal combustion engine and although steam was still taking precedence, internal combustion-powered machines started to make an appearance among farming implements. The innovation really started in America because there was a smaller available workforce than this side of the pond and American fields tended to be much larger than their European counterparts.

In 1892, John Froelich of Iowa built the first successful petrol-powered engine for the farm tractor. At that time, the word 'tractor' had not yet come into usage, but that was what Froelich's machine was.

He pieced together his tractor by mounting a Van Duzen engine on a Robinson steam traction engine chassis and then rigging up his own gearing for propulsion, both backwards and forwards. Froelich found success in using the machine to power a threshing

machine by belt.

Nothing like this had been seen before, and it was many years before other manufacturers caught on with the idea. Froelich, in the meantime, took his tractor to Waterloo in Iowa to show to some businessmen. They were so impressed, they immediately formed a company to manufacture the Froelich tractor, named the company 'The Waterloo Gasoline Traction Engine Company' and made Froelich the president.

The company experimented with farm tractors for some time but it was another 20 years before they began production of what we now know as the Waterloo Boy. The first official model, the 'LA', sold just 20 but it was a step in the right direction, so the company brought out the Model R single-speed tractor in 1914. Farmers liked it and within a year, sales had reached over 100.

By 1918, the year the Model R was discontinued, more than 8,000 had been sold. When the Model 'N' Waterloo Boy, with two forward speeds, was introduced, it proved to be another success and from then on the company put all their efforts into building tractors.

The word 'tractor' was first coined in 1906 by Hart-Parr, a company that had made their first tractor in 1902. The sales manager, WH Williams, is credited with using the term in company advertising. Believing the words 'traction engine' were too vague and too long to be used, he took the Latin verb 'trahere' (to pull) and invented the new term.

By 1905, Hart Parr had become the first company to run a factory solely for the manufacture of tractors. What's more, they started a highly successful school to teach farmers about proper tractor maintenance and operation, and it is for this reason that the company have been given the title Founders of the Tractor Industry.

Many of the early machines were huge and still based on steam engine styling. The trend towards building smaller machines started around 1910, and the pioneer manufacturers of some of the early small tractors include such evocative names as Steel King, Happy Farmer and Farmer Boy. The popularity of tractors was soaring and in America, where there had been just six tractor manufacturers in 1905, the number had increased to more than 160 by 1920.

AFTER STEAM

But problems lay ahead for many of these manufacturers as many became bankrupt as a result of the Wall Street Crash or disappeared altogether in mergers.

The first recorded tractor sale in Britain, to a landowner by the name of Mr Locke-King, took place in September 1897. It involved the oil-burning Hornsby-Ackroyd Patent Safety Oil Traction engine built by Hornsby of Lincoln. This machine weighed in at 8.5 tons and was powered by a Stuart and Binney engine. It was started by means of a blowlamp that created a hotspot in the cylinder head and so allowed the single cylinder engine to fire up without the need for any form of starting mechanism.

Hornsby, which used a 20hp engine with a horizontal cylinder for its tractor, built four of these machines. One of them was exhibited at the Royal Show in 1897 and was awarded the silver medal of the Royal Agricultural Society of England. The Hornsby company supplied various machines to the British War Office and experimented extensively with crawler tracks. The patents that it took out for these tracks were later sold to the Holt Company in America.

However, the first commercially successful design was Englishman Dan Albone's three-wheel Ivel tractor of 1902. Albone was an inventor and bicycle manufacturer who was responsible for the design of the Ivel safety bicycle, but he also decided to branch out into light tractor manufacture. The Ivel tractor had one wheel at the front, two large rear wheels and a water-cooled engine.

Like the Hornsby-Ackroyd, this tractor was a medal winner at the Royal Show and in total more than 500 were built. Unfortunately, not long after Albone's death in 1906, the company ceased production and was no longer a major force in the industry.

Herbert Percy Saunderson was an English blacksmith who decided to change careers and became an agent for Massey-Harris, a Canadian company that specialised in farm machinery. He started off by importing the company's products but then decided to have a go at manufacturing his own machines and formed his own company, the Saunderson Tractor and Implement Company.

His first tractor, a three-wheel machine, was a success but, not content

with this, he moved on to design a four-wheel machine. This tractor, which was unveiled in 1908, had a removable lorry body and so could be used both on the road and for agricultural purposes.

Saunderson moved into the export market, shipped his tractors to Canada, Australia and New Zealand and grew to be the largest tractor manufacturer outside the USA at that time. When World War I started, the Saunderson Tractor and Implement Company was the only company in Britain large enough to meet the increasing demand for tractors.

One big success story during the war years was the Bull Tractor. This was one of the first small and relatively cheap tractors to become available. Little Bull, as it became known, had a power output of 12hp engine whereas its bigger brother, Big Bull, had a 25hp twin cylinder engine. The Bull Tractor Company of Minnesota had instant success with their small tractors and became one of the biggest suppliers of tractors at the time.

Strangely enough, the company did little manufacturing but farmed out orders to a local steel company. Engines from various suppliers were fitted to Bull tractors; supply problems often ensued and once Fordson came into the market Bull could not compete and folded. At its zenith in 1914, Bull was top in tractor sales in the whole of America, yet four years later the company ceased to exist. What happened to Bull also happened to many other firms in the early days of tractor manufacture.

During World War I, Weeks-Dungey entered the market. They were agricultural engineers from Kent but even with their models in the market place, Britain was still short of tractors and these had to be imported, mainly from America. The International Harvester Corporation marketed the models from its range, which they considered were most suited to British farming methods and conditions.

They decided that some of the American names wouldn't suit the British market and so renamed them, the Big Bull being retitled the Whiting Bull, a Parret model being rechristened the Clydesdale and the Waterloo Boy, as we saw previously, being sold in Britain as the Overtime. In addition, the Austin Motor Company offered a Peoria model that it renamed Model 1 Culti Tractor.

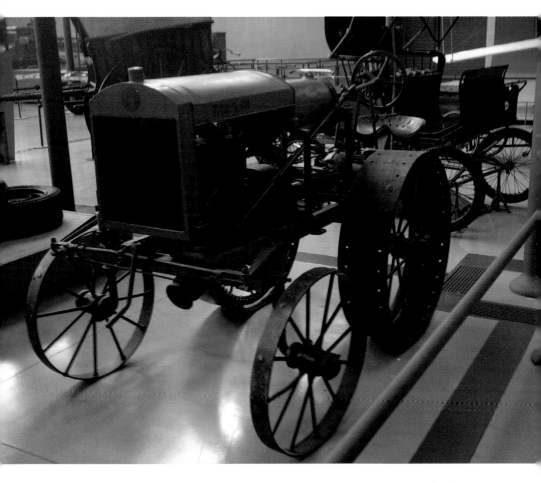

Post WWI

B y the end of World War I in 1918, the tractor had been well and truly accepted as a practical agricultural machine and was seen as the perfect implement for ploughing. A period of prosperity that followed, and the need to boost food production after the war, saw more and more farmers wanting and needing mechanisation on their farms.

The number of tractor manufacturers around the world quickly increased. Henry Ford's company, which was better known for their cars but had entered the tractor market just before the war, was now selling machines in vast numbers and at one point sold 75 per cent of all tractors in America. Ford had started to mass-produce tractors during the war and had sold their first consignment of 7,000, the Fordson F, exclusively to the British government – an order that was fulfilled in seven months.

In the spring of 1918, the Ford company was building 80 farm tractors a day and was hoping to reach 300 a day by the end of the year. By 1920, Ford boasted that they had sold 100,000 tractors and the model F became the most influential and commercially important design in tractor history. Ford's production methods were so successful that other firms either had to copy or go out of business, and many small businesses struggled in vain against the Ford onslaught.

It is estimated that by 1921 in America there were 186 tractor companies, including new names such as Bates, Ebert–Duryea, Kardell and Michigan Utility. In Europe and elsewhere, there were Fiat, Bubba and Landini in Italy, Steyr in Austria, Hofherr and Schrantz (HSCS) in Hungary, Hürliman of Switzerland, Kommunar in what was then the USSR and Ronaldson & Tippet in Australia.

Growing numbers of farmers wanted tractors, so many of these companies started to build budget machines. Specialist budget tractor manufacturers also began to emerge with designs

LEFT
A three-wheeled
tractor in a field
of maize

different to those of the larger machines of the past.

The Glasgow, manufactured by the Scottish firm of Wallace, was a typical three-wheeled machine of its time, with the difference that there were two wheels in the front and a single wheel at the back. All three wheels were driven and no differential was fitted. Instead, a pawl and ratchet system was fitted to the front wheels, which gave maximum grip while at the same time allowing different rotational speeds for turning.

The Glasgow was built between 1918 and 1924 and several were exported, notably to New Zealand. Unfortunately, as with so many other manufacturers, Wallace succumbed to the Fordson price advantage and simple mass production, and manufacture had to cease. Nowadays, 11 of these tractors are known to exist in the world.

In order to compete with Fordson and retain their market shares, other manufacturers were forced to come up with novel ideas. Most companies, like Case and John Deere, cut their prices. The International Harvester Corporation, however, came up with the idea of offering a free plough to

each purchaser of a new tractor. This scheme was a great success and it enabled the company to develop and introduce new models.

In addition to this kind of incentive, all the major manufacturers sought to offer more advanced tractors to their customers. Case, for example, introduced a cast frame tractor with the engine running across the frame, while in 1924 John Deere brought out the Model D, a tractor that had two forward gears and one reverse.

Austin, the car manufacturer, decided to get into tractor manufacturing and although its design was based on the Fordson model, the Austin tractor had a transverse two-speed unit unlike the Fordson, which was fitted with a three-speed inline gearbox. Austin's tractor was powered by a modified 'Heavy 20' car engine and ran on paraffin. It wasn't particularly reliable but, paradoxically, it sold well and remained in production for many years.

The Fordson F had a real stranglehold on the market, but when Ford moved its production out of America and to Cork in Ireland, the Irish inventor Harry Ferguson came

up with plans that would once again change the face of tractor history. Until that time, Ferguson had been selling ploughs, but he realised that he needed to design one that would be specifically suitable for the Fordson F. The result was the Duplex Hitch.

Previously, farm implements had usually been towed behind the tractor just as they had been pulled behind horses for centuries. This system wasn't very efficient and in wet conditions the tractor wheels would slip while the

implement dug in. Ferguson realised that to overcome this problem, the implement needed to be attached to the tractor. He set about designing such a system and in 1925 patented the Duplex Hitch, a two-hitch point system.

Although this had advantages over the previous system, Ferguson was conscious that it could still be improved upon. His design totally revolutionised agriculture and today, 85 per cent of all tractors incorporate an updated form of his revolutionary three-point linkage system.

Innovation

The three-point linkage

When Ferguson set out to design a three-hitch system, hydraulics were not in common use, but he understood that to enable the system to be easy to use, he needed to use this comparatively new technology. Initially, Ferguson designed two upper links and one lower link, but he quickly realised that this caused a problem with the linkage geometry, so he turned his invention upside down so that it consisted of two lower and one upper link.

Previously, the tractor driver had to haul a series of levers, tug on ropes or wind handles in order to attach implements. Now it was a simple task with one control lever as trailed implements were supported by the hydraulic system.

Ferguson received patent No 320084 for his invention in 1928, but he still needed a lightweight tractor to demonstrate its advantages. Although

he had an agreement with Ford, he realised that the only way forward was to build his own tractor and use his own attachments on it.

Together with his engineers, he built a prototype – and he was adamant that he wanted it painted black. The prototype was put to the test: not only did it pull the plough but the hydraulic system allowed the depth of the plough to be controlled from the tractor, and the three-point linkage system, together with larger wheels on the back than on the front, prevented the plough from toppling over if it hit a large stone in the ground.

The prototype was a triumph and full production of the Black Tractor started in 1935. The direct descendant of the Black Tractor was the TE20 (TE Tractor England), lovingly known as the Fergie, that became a common sight on farms all over Britain and the world in the 1940s and early 1950s. David Brown became the manufacturer of the Black Tractor and the colour was subsequently changed to grey, a colour that became synonymous with Ferguson tractors. But it was for a quite mundane reason that the colour was changed – grey was the cheapest colour to produce!

Other makers offering mounted implements found it difficult to use the Ferguson linkage system as Ferguson's dealers naturally gave priority to their company's implements. It was therefore necessary for there to be an alternative. Both David Brown and Fordson offered a range of approved implements to suit their tractors, although there was not a great deal of difference between them and some were in essence interchangeable.

An effort was eventually agreed upon to standardise things and an agreed linkage design was brought out. This enabled tractors from different companies to accommodate implements from other companies.

Pneumatic Tyres

By the 1930s, tractors had become cheap and reasonably reliable, but they were lagging behind cars and bicycles as far as tyres were concerned, as they still ran on solid lugged steel wheels. This meant they were not suitable for use on surfaced roads and were also were not ideal for cultivation purposes, as they caused too much damage to the roots of crops. Solid tyres that were suitable for roads were unsuitable for field use, so an alternative was needed.

One of the first men to experiment with pneumatic tyres had been Charles Goodyear, who in the 1830s purchased the patent rights to a sulphur treatment that helped him in his development of vulcanisation. Goodyear discovered that if the sulphur is removed from rubber and then heated, it will retain its elasticity. In America, Goodrich experimented with a zero-pressure tyre while Firestone tested modified aircraft tyres. These had moulded angled lugs and were inflated to around 15 psi, giving them enough flexibility to cope with uneven surfaces.

These tyres met the various needs of the farm tractor and they became a great success. By the late 1930s, around half of all tractors sold were fitted with pneumatic tyres and by 1940 nearly all machines were sold with rubber tyres. Tests showed that a tractor fitted with rubber tyres was easier to steer, capable

of travelling at much higher speeds, had improved fuel economy and was far more versatile.

With the tractor becoming so versatile, the use of the horse in farming declined rapidly. In 1925, there were approximately 23 million draught horses and fewer than half a million tractors in use on Britain's farms yet 20 years later the number of horses had halved while the number of tractors had more than quadrupled.

Crawler Tractors

The first experiments with tracked machinery go back to the Middle Ages, but the first serious examples can be attributed to Richard Edgeworth, born in 1744. Edgeworth's scientific interests led him in various directions, including an early form of a steam-driven caterpillar system. His machine consisted of a single continuous metal belt that enabled it to move more easily over uneven terrain. A limited number were used in the Crimean War.

It wasn't until the 1870s that a proper crawler tractor appeared. The Russian peasant Fyodor Abramovich Blinov patented "the special carriage with endless rails for transportation of cargo along highways and roads". Blinov had started his career as a stoker on river boats but not a lot else is known about his early history and his interest in carriages. By 1877 he had built his carriage with caterpillar tracks, a vehicle that had no engine and was pulled by horses.

A year later, he applied for a patent which was granted in 1879, and the next few years saw him experimenting with tracked tractors and ultimately building a steam model, but no one was interested in his invention.

In 1886, the American lawyer Charles Dinsmoor, received patent No 351,749 for his tracked vehicle which, it is believed, he sold to the Holt Company. Indeed, tracked machinery was pioneered by Benjamin Holt in the early 1900s but World War I speeded up the development of crawler technology, first with the tank and then with the tractor.

By the 1940s, half track – that is regular wheels on the front for steering, and tracks on the back to propel the vehicle and carry most of the load – were evolving.

LEFT A Caterpillar crawler tractor

4x4 tractors

During the 1920s, much experimentation took place in an effort to find an alternative to tracked tractors, but it wasn't until after World War II that various companies offered four-wheel drive conversions to many of their tractors. Admittedly this was using surplus stock from the war, but it was something that appealed to farmers.

With 4WD becoming increasingly popular, more manufacturers started to offer their machines in 2 or 4WD configurations. The 1950s saw difficulties for tractor manufacturers on both sides of the Atlantic and many of the companies who had made conversion were soon out of business.

The Green Shoots Of Recovery

The Wall Street Crash of 1929 and the general downturn in the economy both in Britain and America in the 1930s meant that many agricultural machinery manufacturers went out of business leaving, after mergers and takeovers, just a few strong companies.

With the outbreak of World War II, it became obvious that these few companies would not be able to meet the needs of the British farmers in their efforts to feed the nation. The decision was made to import American tractors, many of them coming to Britain thanks to the Lend-Lease programme. This was a scheme enacted in 1941 and devised to enable Britain and other Allied nations to have supplies of equipment that would otherwise not have been available.

Allis-Chalmers, John Deere, Caterpillar and Oliver, were among the manufacturers who became household names in Britain. Ford already had its plant in Ireland, and they continued to manufacture tractors in considerable numbers, although they did redesign their machines in order to use less metal.

Another aspect of the war that affected tractor design briefly was the conflict in South East Asia, which limited rubber supplies. For a short period, steel wheels came back into use.

In the years immediately after the war, Britain needed a lot of help to rebuild the country, money was still tight and few farmers were prepared or able to splash out on new machinery yet, there was naturally a need to maximise food production. Generous guaranteed prices were fixed for certain crops and there was Government support for investment. This enabled many farmers to purchase the latest equipment and use rising quantities of fertilisers and pesticides.

ABOVE
Allis-Chalmers
tractor. Credit
Charles01

Farming bounced back as production soared in the following decades. Farming was becoming increasingly mechanised, fields were getting larger and by the 1960s there were few horses left working on British farms. This was the start of Britain's second agricultural revolution.

Tractor Trials

From the beginning, tractor manufacturers in search of sales had a tendency to exaggerate the capabilities of their machines. Tractor trials were instituted in order to put an end to this practice and to allow for realistic comparisons to be made between various makes and models.

The idea for official tractor testing was formulated in Canada and several states in America, but for a long time there was nothing official. By 1907, tractors powered by the internal combustion engine were making an appearance and there was much competition between these new machines and steam-powered ones. The Grieg brothers of Winnipeg, Manitoba organised a series of tests, which we now know as the Winnipeg trials.

The tests between the two types of tractor showed up the limitations of steam tractors and the results allowed farmers to better judge the suitability of machines and what kind to purchase. Although the Winnipeg trials were an important milestone in tractor testing, it was the Nebraska trials that really prevented manufacturers from making overinflated claims.

In 1916, a farmer called Wilmot Crozier found himself with a Ford Tractor Company tractor (not connected to the Henry Ford Company) with which he was very unhappy. Crozier had hoped that his new-fangled purchase would be a wonderful replacement for his team of horses, but it gave him nothing but trouble, with poor handling and power. He demanded a replacement from Ford but the new machine proved no better.

A few years later, Crozier was elected to the Nebraska State Legislature and in 1919 he sponsored a bill to make tractor testing mandatory in the state. This test would mean no new tractor model could be sold without a permit, and that could only be obtained after one of the tractors had been tested at the University Of Nebraska Agricultural

TRACTOR TRIALS

Engineering Department.

So, the Nebraska Tractor Test Laboratory (NTTL) was established, with test examining fuel consumption, horse power and engine efficiency. There were also practical tests that gauged the tractor's performance with implements on a draw bar. The results had to match up to the manufacturer's published claims; in fact, the law decreed that manufacturers had to print all or none of the test results on their publicity material.

The first tractor scheduled for testing was a Twin City 12–20, but a heavy snowfall meant testing had to be postponed until the following spring. As a result of the snowstorm, the first tractor actually tested was a Waterloo Boy Model N. The test ran from March 31 to April 9, 1920, and the engineers discovered the Waterloo Boy performed erratically, but they did not disqualify the tractor. That year the engineering department tested 69 models.

Over the years, with changes in technology, there have been many changes to the test. In the 1960s, for example, the minimum advertised horsepower for tractors to be tested was 20hp but by the 1980s this had risen to 40hp. The tests for one tractor usually take a week and they can only be done when air temperatures are above 10 degrees and below 21 degrees Celsius. This is because performance changes according to prevailing atmospheric conditions.

In Great Britain, the first tractor trials were held at Benson, Oxfordshire in 1930, and the World Agricultural Tractor Trials, as they became known, were a massive turning point in the history of British tractors.

As in Nebraska, all tractors brought to the trials were put through a series of tests as well as ploughing trials in the field. These trials attracted a variety of interest from predominantly British and American tractor manufacturers, including Fordson, Roadless, Case and Massey–Harris, as well as a few European ones such as Linke from Germany and Latil from France. In total, 36 machines were brought to the first trial.

Ironically, one of the failures at this trial was the Fordson Model N, which went on to become one of the most successful tractors of all time.

Pioneers
And Innovators

Allis-Chalmers

Allis-Chalmers can trace their roots back to the 1840s, when they were involved in mining, steam engines and other industrial equipment. The original company, known as Edward P Allis and Company, was built up by EP Allis of New York after acquiring a shop called the Reliance Works. Although the company had no experience in building tractors, they realised they needed to diversify and that the future lay in this kind of machinery.

In 1914, Allis-Chalmers built their first tractor, a tricycle design with a 15-30hp engine. This tractor was started on gasoline but, once the engine warmed up, it ran on the cheaper kerosene. At this time, Allis-Chalmers did not sell through a dealership network, although they did have a mail order catalogue. From 1928 to 1933, the Cockshutt Company distributed Allis-Chalmers and United tractors, as at that time they did not have a tractor design of their own.

In 1929, Allis-Chalmers joined the United Tractor and Equipment Corporation to produce the United tractor as part of a wide range of farm machinery. The United Tractor and Equipment Corporation was made up of some 30 other companies but, unfortunately, it did not last long. One good thing that emerged from the Corporation, though, was the highly respected Allis U.

The Allis-Chalmers Model U became famous as the first production farm tractor offered with pneumatic rubber tyres. Until then, all tractors had used plain steel wheels that had limited road speed, but the U could reach an impressive 15mph. At first, the Model U was fitted with a Continental

L-head side valve engine but from 1933 onwards Allis-Chalmers produced their own 34hp overhead valve four-cylinder UM engine. This popular Allis-Chalmers tractor was built from 1929 until 1952 and it was probably the best-liked of the company's tractors to be imported into Britain.

PIONEERS AND INNOVATORS

At this time, Allis–Chalmers decided to introduce a distinctive colour scheme to their tractors; the previous colour had been a dull green. The change in livery was made so that customers could immediately differentiate Allis–Chalmers's tractors from other makes and also so that they could be seen easily in the countryside even when they were caked in mud. The colour chosen was Persian Orange, a strikingly vivid hue that in the 1960s was changed to Persian Orange No 2, an even brighter shade.

Over the years, Allis–Chalmers were responsible for many acquisitions, including in 1928 the Monarch Tractor Company, a manufacturer of caterpillar tractors; in 1931, Advance-Rumely, based in LaPorte, Indiana, a manufacturer of threshing machines and large tractors; and in the 1950s, the Buda Engine Company, the Gleaner Harvester Company, the Tractomotive Corporation and the French company Vendeuvre. These acquisitions enabled Allis–Chalmers to become the fourth largest manufacturer of agricultural machinery in America.

In 1939, the company introduced the Model B, the first in a long line of highly successful small lightweight and relatively cheap tractors. The Model B sold in excess of 100,000 during its lifetime and those numbers included an industrial version, the IB, which the sales literature at the time proudly claimed "drives like a car as it has similar controls with a foot-controlled throttle, clutch, and brake. In addition there are individual handbrakes on each rear wheel."

One Allis–Chalmers models that followed, the WD tractor, was brimming with new ideas. There were so many new features and improvements on the WD that the sales force were obliged to learn a whole new set of terms for the tractor. The WD was the first tractor to feature power-adjustable rear wheels, single hitch-point implements, traction-booster and two–clutch power control. The last feature allowed the operator to stop the drive wheels while power continued to the PTO (power take off) operating implements like combines and balers.

Production of the WD began in 1948 and lasted for six years. The D series of tractors replaced the whole of Allis-Chalmers' previous line-up, a range of more than 50 models.

The company was to prove

innovative in 1959, when they experimented with fuel cells on the D12 model. They chose propane mixed with other gases and the fuel was carried in pressurised containers and supplied a bank of 1,008 fuel cells that occupied almost the entire space under the bonnet. The electricity generated powered a 20hp motor. The tractor never went into production but Allis-Chalmers maintained a research programme into fuel cells for a number of years.

The D series was the last Allis-Chalmers tractor commonly seen in Britain. During the 1980s, the company started to struggle in a difficult economic climate and in 1985 they were forced to sell their farming equipment division to Klockner-Humboldt-Deutz of Germany, which was renamed Deutz-Allis. They in turn became part of the AGCO group. All production of Allis-Chalmers tractors ceased and the company officially closed its offices in January 1999.

In 2008, Briggs & Stratton Power Products announced that they would build a series of lawn and garden tractors under the Allis-Chalmers brand name

Case

As International Harvester became part of the large conglomerate of Case in the 1980s, it seemed a natural progression for Case to look at their machines. Case were very innovative in their early days but they got caught up in design doldrums and for a long period failed to keep up with the latest trends, before coming out of their depression and becoming a force to be reckoned with again.

Jerome Increase Case founded the company that bore his name in 1847. He started out by manufacturing steam engines before moving on to steam traction engines and, eventually, internal combustion tractors. By 1912, Case had a commercially successful tractor on the market and in the next seven years, he introduced eight new designs, all with transverse engines. Probably the most famous of these is the Crossmotor, a series of three- and four-wheeled, water-cooled, four-cylinder machines that Case stuck with for the following decade.

By 1929, Case decided to change the engine alignment and moved to a longitudinally mounted engine with the Model L and the identical but smaller

Model C. The Model L was a hit with farmers in America and when it was brought to England for the tractor trials at Benson, the British public fell in love with its excellent fuel economy. It became a great success.

Throughout the 1930s, more models came out of the Case factory at Racine, Wisconsin. During World War II, Case built more than 15,000 specialised and modified military tractors for the American and Allied forces. By the time the war ended, though, Case models were looking outdated and though they also had the Farmall, there was little other choice for farmers. We will learn more about Farmall later in this chapter.

In addition, just as the war ended in 1945, there was a 440-day strike at the Racine plant, causing Case to lose even more market share, and profits continued to decline through the early 1950s. Major management restructuring had to take place and, with a new team on board, Case released a multitude of new or improved implements, including the 500 series.

The 500 had an inline six-cylinder, fuel-injected, diesel engine, power steering and a push-button start, but it was still basically a re-engineered Model L. Things were looking very bleak for Case and they were on the verge of bankruptcy when they decided to diversify into industrial equipment.

Things did not improve much in the following years, although Case acquired a number of companies including the American Tractor Corporation in 1957, the French company of Société

Française, Vierzon in 1960 and David Brown Tractors in 1972. This was beneficial to Case as they now had an opportunity to expand into previously difficult markets.

From 1972 onwards, David Brown tractors were painted in their white livery while Case's machines were done out in Case Red. Case itself had changed ownership in the 1960s, becoming part of the Kern County Land Company (KCL) of California, which in turn became part of Tenneco. Tenneco dropped many of the Case lines and things started to improve, especially in America's bicentennial year of 1976.

In that year, Case produced a red, white and blue special edition tractor, a Case 1570 called the 'Spirit of 76'. This tractor was the most powerful two-wheel drive tractor of its time with a 7800cc turbocharged diesel engine. Unfortunately for Case, a time of recession came in the 1980s and there was a deepening farm depression.

But the company's losses started to come down as they cut the workforce and in 1999 they agreed to be acquired by New Holland, a subsidiary of Fiat. Case New Holland (CNH) was formed

but this company continued to make losses and in 2004 the decision was made to close the manufacturing plants in Racine.

Nowadays, Case manufacture tractors from 60-608hp. These latest machines, the Quadtrac and the Steiger, have been built to reflect new emission legislation effective from 2011.

David Brown

David Brown came into building tractors by accident, as we saw earlier. Prior to his involvement with Harry Ferguson, his company had been concerned with gear cutting. Once Brown realised that building tractors could be a profitable enterprise, he started to build them to his own design,

with the VAK-1 being the first.

The VAK-1 was introduced in 1939 and was first shown at the 100th Royal Show at Windsor. Although it was similar to the Ferguson, it was considerably larger and more powerful. Many were built during the war for military purposes, mainly for the RAF, which used them to tow aircraft and bomb trolleys. But the machine that really brought the David Brown name into the tractor world was the legendary Cropmaster, launched in 1947.

With the Cropmaster, the company introduced the policy of including as standard specification items that had previously been regarded as extras. These included hydraulic lift, swing drawbar

and electric lighting, which consisted of one offside front headlight and one rear light. The Cropmaster also featured a wind deflector, which was unique on tractors at that time.

The styling of most of David Brown's tractors was based on the VAK-1 until the 900 series was revealed in 1956 at the Smithfield Show. The 900 was available with four alternative engines: diesel – 40bhp; TVO (kerosene) – 37bhp; petrol – 40bhp; and high compression petrol (gasoline) – 45bhp. At this time the colour scheme was changed to a rather distinctive red bodywork and wheel hubs with pale blue wheels and grille.

The early 1960s saw the launch of the 880 Implematic, known as the 880C and 880D models, again with a change in the colour scheme. The early ones were painted red with yellow trim and wheels. The Implematic was powered by a four-cylinder diesel engine of 42.5hp and transmission was via a six forward and two reverse speed gearbox. Hydraulics were available as an optional extra. One thing that distinguished the Implematic from all the tractors that had gone before it was that it was the first one to have a negative earth electrical system to comply with European standards.

Between 1967 and 1971, David Brown produced the Selectamatic, with yet another change in the colour scheme, to winter white and chocolate brown. The early Selectamatics were powered by a three-cylinder diesel engine with transmission via 12 forward and four reverse gears. The tractor's hydraulic system allowed the driver to select depth and height control. Later models were to see an increase in power output as a result of a request from

farmers to have more horsepower.

In 1972, the company was acquired by Tenneco, owners of the Case Group. The David Brown name continued to be used until 1983, when the Case 94 series was launched. The very last tractor to be built at the David Brown works in Meltham, Yorkshire was a Case 1594 that rolled off the production line in 1988.

Caterpillar

The Caterpillar Company was formed in the late 19th century by Benjamin Holt and Daniel Best, who had previously competed against each other to build caterpillar tractors for use in farming. Although tracked tractors were heavier and not so easy to handle as wheeled models, they did work well in heavy, wet soils.

Holt and Best realised that they could not work independently of each other so in 1925 the two companies – the Holt Manufacturing Company of Stockton, California and the CL Best Gas Traction Company of San Leandro, California – merged to form the Caterpillar Tractor Company. They based themselves in Peoria, Illinois, where the Caterpillar headquarters still remain.

Immediately after the merger, the two men had to decide which tractors in their respective line-ups they were going to keep. Best's large 30 and 60 were retained and were rebadged Caterpillar, but Holt's 5 and 10 ton machines were unwanted as they were very expensive to build and rather outdated.

All of Caterpillar's early tractors ran on petrol (gasoline in America) and were painted grey. It wasn't until late 1931 that the company took the decision to paint all their new tractors bright yellow with black trim, a colour scheme that has continued to this day.

Also around this time, Caterpillar started to experiment with diesel engines and had its first prototype ready for testing. Diesel proved far more

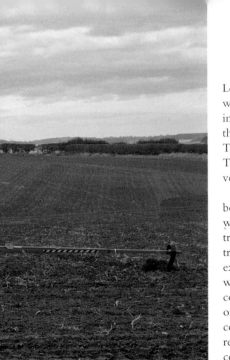

Lease agreement. After the war there was a huge road–building programme in the UK and in 1950, in the first of their foreign operations, the Caterpillar Tractor Company set up in Britain. This was followed in 1963 with a joint venture with Mitsubishi of Japan.

By the 1980s, Caterpillar were being overtaken by producers of four-wheel drive tractors. Their crawler tractors were slow because of their steel tracks, and so the company started to experiment with rubber tracks, which would be not only faster but also considerably quieter. After thousands of hours of testing, a tractor with a continuous rubber belt was finally released. The Challenger 65, a water-cooled six-cylinder machine powered by a Cat diesel engine, went into production in 1987 and over the years various models of the original concept have been released.

In Europe, Caterpillar completed a deal with Claas of Germany, an agricultural machinery manufacturer, whereby Claas would market Challenger tractors under their own name and in their colours of green and white. In 2002, AGCO began to produce

economical, although at that time the fuel itself was of a poor quality. By the mid–1930s, Caterpillar had a complete range of diesel tractors, from the small RD 4 through to the RD8 with horsepower of 118.

Like several other manufacturers during World War II, Caterpillar shipped many tractors, mainly the D6 and D7, to Britain under the Lend-

Challenger tracked machines under licence from Caterpillar and over recent years have expanded the Challenger name into a full line of farm machinery.

John Deere

John Deere is now the world's largest maker of farm and forestry equipment and have tractors ranging from 53 to 450hp. The company started out in 1837 and is the only US tractor maker still in business under its original name.

John Deere, a blacksmith from Vermont living in Illinois, noticed that the cast iron ploughs the settlers brought with them from the eastern United States couldn't cope with the thicker, stickier soil of the Midwest prairies.

after his first plough, he was producing 1,000 products a year. At that time, Deere promised: "I will never put my name on a product that does not have in it the best that is in me."

It was not until 1914 that the company branched out into tractors with the purchase of the Waterloo Gasoline Engine Company. They were already producing a 25hp machine, the Waterloo Boy, and it was a name that the John Deere Company kept until 1923 with the introduction of the Model D – the first tractor to bear the John Deere name.

The decision was made to produce a horizontally mounted, two-cylinder engine to run on kerosene although it was started on petrol. With just two forward and one reverse gear, this was quite a basic machine and so relatively affordable. The Model D had the longest run of any make or model of John Deere tractor, being in production for 30 years. Incidentally, all John Deere two-cylinder tractors were called 'Johnny Poppers' or 'Poppin' Johnnies' owing to their distinctive exhaust note.

The biggest machine that John Deere ever built was the Model R. This was

Farmers had to stop every few feet to scrape the clay off the blades, so Deere set about designing and ultimately making a polished steel plough. When it appeared in 1836, it was an immediate sensation and it became the first commercially successful steel plough in America.

Deere's business thrived and ten years

the first tractor with a diesel engine, which made it cheaper to run than any of its rivals; in fact, when it was tested at Nebraska, the Model R set an all-time record for fuel economy. Another first for this tractor was that it was the first to be fitted with a cab.

After years of manufacturing two-cylinder tractors, John Deere switched to four- and six-cylinder machines, and there followed a succession of new machines – the 10 series – ranging in power from 35 to 80hp. They were swiftly followed by the 20 series and then in the 1970s the 30 and 40 series. Of the 30 series, the 4430 was almost certainly the most popular. It had a proper enclosed cab with tinted windows and was considered quiet enough in use for a stereo radio cassette machine to be fitted

Diversification continued, and in 1992 a whole new design series was brought out in the 6000 and 7000. Most but not all of the components were new and the tractors featured entirely new engines, which were now made by Deere. The 7000 series had some more new features that made the driver's life much more comfortable: better visibility,

RIGHT
A selection of
Farmall tractors.
Credit Dual Freq

an air-cushioned seat and an instrument
panel that tilted with the steering wheel.

Launches of new models continued
throughout the 2000s. The latest
products to come out of the John Deere
factory are the 8R/8RT Series tractors.
Despite a 9L engine, they set a new
record at the Nebraska tests with an
all-time record for fuel economy. These
tractors come with 16 forward and five
reverse gears and more than 20 lights for
round-the-clock usage.

Although John Deere are American
manufacturers, they have factories
throughout the world and distribute their
products in more than 150 countries.

Farmall

The International Harvester Company
(IH) was formed by an amalgamation of
the McCormick Harvesting Machine
Company and the Deering Harvester
Company in July 1902. The company
went on to become the largest tractor
manufacturer in the world, and some of
their most successful machines were sold
under the Farmall machine.

The Farmall name was initially used
on a model but ultimately it came to
be seen as a brand. The first Farmall

machine was seven years in the making
and it emerged in 1924. IH needed to
build a machine that would be a threat

to the success of Fordson, and the Farmall Regular was just that. It sparked a revolution in tractor design.

Until the introduction of this tractor, machines had been single-purpose: they could either plough or cultivate but not

do both. This tricycle-style (with two big wheels in the back and two small wheels next to each other in the front) multi-purpose machine could plough, thresh and shred; many jobs that had formerly been done by hand.

It was such an innovative concept that IH were concerned the farming public would not accept the machine, so initially, to avoid any embarrassment, it was sold as a loss leader purely in the state of Texas. But to IH's great relief it sold well and went into full production, with the tricycle configuration influencing the industry for the next half century. In fact, the Farmall Regular sold more than the rest of the IH range put together.

Over the next few years, larger and more powerful tractors came off the Rock Island, Illinois factory, starting with the Increased-Power Farmall, or F-20, in 1932. This was in essence just an upgraded Regular, although it had a four-speed gearbox unlike the Regular three-speeds. Almost 150,000 F-20s were built.

IH continued to manufacture the F series until 1938, with most of the tractors being slightly updated versions of ones that had gone before. One change the company made was to change their paint colour from a dark bluey grey to Farmall red in 1936 when tractor styling started to become a principal issue.

IH employed an industrial designer, Richard Loewy – who later designed some Studebaker cars – to design a tractor and he came up with the Farmall A, or Culti-Vision. This four-cylinder tractor was another radical Farmall design with its engine offset to the left by 20cm while the driver sat to the right with a totally unobstructed view ahead.

After the war, IH introduced what became known as the 'Super Series'. With this series, the company added a touch control hydraulic lift system as a standard feature, along with electric starting and lights. The 'Super Series' enjoyed good sales but IH were concerned about competitors so in 1954 another new series was brought out.

This number series, starting with the 200, featured the groundbreaking 'Hydra-Creeper' system, which allowed the tractor to operate at very slow speeds: down to 0.25 mph. Later, this option was fitted to other tractors in the series.

But IH were struggling and sales were slumping as the company failed to keep up with the latest innovations. They then went down the line of producing big six-cylinder models.

In July 1958, the IH office in Illinois invited 12,000 dealers from more than 25 countries to examine their 60 series, including the first large six-cylinder 460 and 560 models. Unfortunately, many of these tractors were breaking down

in the field and had to be recalled. This disaster allowed IH's competitors to take advantage of the recall and IH lost even more customers.

Throughout the 1960s and 1970s, IH continued to introduce new Farmall tractors and they employed all manner of marketing strategies to try to make a success, but although they did produce some lasting machines, the good times were over. The very last Farmall of any kind rolled off the production line in 1974 and the name Farmall disappeared entirely in 1975.

In 1985, International Harvester merged with JI Case and all their equipment was manufactured under that name. Ironically, Case have recently revived the Farmall brand on some of their modern utility tractors, and the name lives on in four new models.

Fendt

So far, most of tractors we have looked at have been manufactured in either Britain or America, but the Fendt range came out of Germany. Xaver Fendt and Company was founded in 1937 by the two Fendt brothers, Xaver and Paul, who under the guidance of their father, Johann Georg, started to build tractors in a blacksmith's workshop.

They built the very first European small tractor, which had a 6hp engine and was called the Fendt Dieselross. It was little more than a stationary engine with a simple transmission system and wheels, but just a year later the 1,000th

Dieselross, a 16hp F 18, came off the production line. With World War II came fuel shortages, and Fendt developed a gas-powered tractor that would burn practically any combustible material.

Over the years that followed, the Dieselross came out in many forms and horsepower ratings. In 1961, the 100,000th Fendt tractor, a Farmer 2, rolled off the production line. In the mid-70s Fendt introduced the Favorit range and the following decade the

Farmer range came out. The Farmer 300 featured the new feature of a rubber-supported cab. In addition, the 300 was a fast tractor for its time, with a top speed of around 25mph.

In the 90s, further Favorit tractors were introduced, including the 500 C Series, whose models were capable of reaching speeds of 30mph. The 1990s also saw the premiere of the Vario 900 series with the launch of the 926 in 1995. This was the very first heavy duty tractor with the revolutionary, truly stepless Fendt Vario transmission.

A milestone occurred in Fendt's history when it became part of the AGCO group in 1997 and in 2009, the company presented a range of speciality tractors, the Vario 200 series. The V model is a traditional narrow vineyard tractor – the F is wide and the P is wider still – that is aimed at hop- and fruit-growing customers. All of these tractors have a wide range of optional equipment and can be tailor-made to the customer's specifications.

A Fendt tractor, the 828 Vario, was awarded the honour of Tractor of the Year 2011 at the EIMA trade exhibition in Bologna, Italy.

Harry Ferguson

The man whose company bears his name was born in November 1884 in Northern Ireland. As a young boy he tinkered with cars and bicycles, and then he started to invent things, including a powered flying machine that he himself flew – the first of its kind in Ireland.

By 1911 he had opened his own car business, but Ferguson then decided to expand into tractors and ploughs and started to sell American-made tractors. He found them heavy and difficult to manoeuvre, so he designed and built a new kind of plough that was attached to a tractor by the three-point linkage system. Ferguson then set about building his own tractor, the Black Tractor prototype, but his strength was really as an inventor and he needed to team up with a manufacturer.

David Brown of Huddersfield had already been supplying him with components for the Black Tractor and following negotiations, an agreement was reached whereby David Brown would build the tractors and Ferguson would see to the sales side. One aspect of the deal that Ferguson wasn't keen on was the change of colour from black to grey – a colour that we now recognise as the established Ferguson colour.

Ferguson's next partner was Henry Ford, who agreed to mass-produce a tractor with a Ferguson hitch conversion and, once again, Ferguson would market the product. This agreement became known as the 'handshake' agreement as it involved neither paperwork nor lawyers. The tractor that was produced as a result of the deal was the 9N and, although it sold in vast numbers, Ford lost money on each and every one and

PIONEERS AND INNOVATORS

many years later the agreement was ended in a multi-million dollar lawsuit.

The agreement with Ford had only covered North America, and Ferguson wanted to find a company closer to home to build tractors for him. This time he turned to the Standard Motor Company, who in the post-war years were developing a new engine for their family car, the Vanguard. Ferguson decided this engine could be adapted to fit his tractor, an updated version of the 9N which was renamed the TE20 or, more affectionately, the 'Little Grey Fergie'. The Little Grey Fergie's launch was something to behold. In a publicity stunt, Harry Ferguson himself drove the tractor down the steps within Claridge's Hotel in London, an act that was recreated on the 60th anniversary of the tractor.

By 1949, Ferguson had a three-quarters market share of tractor sales in Britain, a figure that is surprising considering that in the first year of production only 315 tractors were manufactured. But by the end of production of all TE20s including variants, more than half a million had been built.

Before signing up in 1952 with his fourth and final partner, Massey-Harris, Ferguson bought a site in Detroit, Michigan, where he started to manufacture his TO 20 (Tractor Overseas), a machine almost identical to the TE20. The merger with Massey-Harris brought together the best of skills from both sides of the Atlantic and an entity that could have become, but didn't, one of the most powerful in tractor production.

Things didn't look good when the Massey-Harris Pony was painted in Ferguson grey and sold through Ferguson dealers while the Ferguson 35, an update of the Little Grey Fergie, was stretched and repainted as the Massey-Harris 50. This left potential buyers totally confused and a breakdown in brand loyalty ensued.

The two companies realised the problems this was causing and ultimately unified their range into Massey-Fergusons, with new corporate colours of red bodywork and grey chassis. The first 'unified' products were referred to as MF25, MF35 and so on, with the numbering referring to the horsepower.

Ferguson's personal links with the company were to prove short-

lived, and within a year he had sold his shareholding and resigned. He didn't give up the idea of constructing another tractor, but due to the economic climate it came to nothing, so he devoted the final years of his life to developing four-wheel drive systems for Grand Prix cars.

The project, known as P99, was eventually developed into a car for driver Stirling Moss, who won at Oulton Park in 1961, the only time a 4WD car has won a Grand Prix – after that win, 4WD was banned. Harry Ferguson did not live to see this achievement as he died in 1960.

Fiat

Not many people associate the name Fiat with tractors, but they are one of the largest tractor manufacturers, not only in Italy but throughout the world. Fiat (Fabbrica Italiana Automobili Torino) was founded by Giovanni Agnelli and had begun to develop tractors by 1910 but, thanks to World War I, it wasn't until 1918 that Fiat unveiled their first prototype.

A year later, the 702 started to roll off the production line. This was a four-cylinder 30hp model that stayed in production for five years. With three forward gears and one reverse, the 702 gained a reputation for being reliable as well as a good workhorse. It was built on an industrial scale and was exported to many countries in Europe, Australia, North and South America.

In 1924, the 702 was replaced by the 703, an even more powerful machine with an engine that came out of one of Fiat's 3.5 ton lorries. But these early Fiats cost more than five times the Fordson price and so were not commercially viable. In 1926 Fiat made the decision to produce a lightweight tractor, which became known as the

700. Throughout its long life, the 700 came out in various guises including, for a time, a crawler version.

The Fiat 55 was introduced in 1950. This too was a crawler tractor, but it was far more powerful, with a 6500cc, four-cylinder diesel engine. The 6 volt electrical system was reliant on a dynamo as there was no battery.

In 1957, Fiat launched its Model 18 La Piccola, and two years later came the 411 – and both these models helped to establish Fiat as a serious tractor manufacturer. In 1962 Fiat signed a licence agreement with the Turkish tractor manufacturer Türk Traktor of Ankara and in 1965, production of Türk Fiyat-branded tractors was started. The following year, more than 2,500 tractors were produced.

The success of the Türk Fiyat joint venture encouraged Fiat to enter into deals with other companies, and they included SIMIT, a leading excavator manufacturer, and in 1974 Allis-Chalmers. The company then became known as Fiat-Allis.

During the 1970s, Fiat-Allis brought out its first 100hp wheeled tractor, the 1000, and then the 150hp 1300. Both these tractors were 4X4 and featured 12 forward and four reverse gears. Fiat claimed to be the largest producers of 4WD tractors in the world.

Further joint ventures were entered into, including agreements with Hitachi, Kobelco, Steyr. Case and Ford New Holland, and these made up the agricultural sector of CNH (Case New Holland) Global. Most of the Fiat group's tractors were sold under the Case and New Holland names, although the group did sell the Steyr brand in Europe.

In early 2011 CNH, together with the truck manufacturer Iveco, was demerged into Fiat Industrial; the reason being that Fiat wanted to create distinct groups within its large company. Only time will tell if groundbreaking tractors will continue to come out of the Fiat group.

Fordson

Henry Ford grew up on a farm outside Detroit and therefore had an interest in the agricultural business. He founded the Ford Motor Company and, as we know, the Model T proved the start of tremendous success in the automotive industry.

But all the time he was working on

cars, Ford was also dabbling in tractor design. When things reached prototype stage, the Ford Motor Company and its directors proved completely unwilling to produce a tractor, so Ford decided to go it alone. At this time, during World War I, food and manpower were in short supply and one of the answers to these problems came in the form of a cheap, mass-produced tractor.

The Fordson Model F first came off the production line in 1917 in limited numbers. The Model F was revolutionary first and foremost because it was above all else a lighter, simpler and easier to understand design than many of the tractors produced by other companies at the time. In addition, it was much cheaper and enabled many farmers to buy their first tractor.

But Henry Ford started to lose interest in tractors and concentrate all his efforts on his cars, so tractor production was shifted to Cork in Ireland in 1919. With the shift to Ireland, it was realised that the Model F needed updating, and the Model N, with a bigger engine, was born.

Within the range, the 8N was the first Ford tractor to feature a clutch on

The sign on the wagon reads:

FORDSON TRACTOR
— MOVES THE EARTH —
→ SHOW US YOUR JOB ←

SOLD BY
PARKWAY MOTOR Co.
1065 WIS. AVE. N.W.

the left side and independent brakes on the right. But Ireland was not a great success story as it was too far from the big tractor markets of England, so production moved once again, this time to Ford's plant in Dagenham, Essex.

In the spring of 1945, the Fordson Major was introduced to British farmers, with Ford giving it the designation E27N: E for English, 27 for 27hp, and N for tractor. Powered by either a Perkins P4 or P6 diesel engine, it was well received and more than 233,000 were built between 1945 and 1952. Following the Major came the Dexta, Power Major, Super Major, and Super Dexta.

In 1959, Ford introduced the Select-O-Speed transmission system, which was supposed to provide the tractor with a wide range of options with ten forward speeds and two reverse. To start with there were innumerable problems with the transmission that Ford had to work on but unfortunately, even though the issues were resolved, Select-O-Speed earned a reputation for being unreliable.

The Super Dexta and Super Major were the last tractors to bear the Fordson name in the 1960s. In 1964, the Fordson brand was discontinued and all

tractors thereafter made by the company, whether in Europe or America, carried the Ford name.

In 1986, Ford expanded its tractor business when it purchased New Holland and two years later it bought the Canadian firm of Versatile.

Nonetheless, in 1991, Fiat acquired Ford New Holland and an agreement was made that they had to cease using the Ford name by 2000.

JCB

JCB is a name that we associate with excavators, but we shouldn't forget that the company has more recently branched out into agricultural machines with its Fastrac and compact tractor ranges.

The Fastrac tractor is a modern high-speed machine. Production of the first Fastrac 100 began in 1990 and since

then the machine has evolved through to the latest Fastrac 3000 Series Xtra, which came out in 2010. All tractors in the Fastrac series feature a two-man cab with full-size seats for the driver and passenger, and in some models there is optional extras of a heated driver's seat, adjustable steering column and air conditioning.

The first Fastrac to feature a Cummins engine was the 185 in 1994; now all Fastracs are fitted with them, most with the QSB 6.7 engine. Some Fastrac models can reach speeds up to 50mph. Braking comes with large external disc brakes on each wheel and air trailer couplings. Many Fastracs are also fitted with ABS.

The most powerful JCB tractor ever is the 260hp 8250 with a Cummins 8.3 engine. This tractor, which has been legally classed as a high-speed tractor, meets latest Tier 3 emissions criteria despite its powerful engine. Other features include eight front and six rear work lights, heated front and rear screens as well as heated electric mirrors and full front and rear suspension. In 2007, the 8250 was awarded the Royal Agricultural Society of England's Gold Medal, with the judges describing it as a "huge leap forward in tractor engineering".

Landini

Landini, a name that is not too well known in Britain, is nevertheless the oldest tractor manufacturer in Italy. The company was founded by Giovanni Landini, a blacksmith apprentice who set up his own business in 1884 in Fabbrico, a wine-growing region of northern Italy.

Business prospered for the young Landini and he decided to branch out into manufacturing items for local farms. First he produced winemaking equipment, then steam and internal combustion engines.

In 1910, Landini built his first fixed hot bulb (Testa Calda) engine, which relied on a hot spot to ignite the fuel. They could run on many fuels and were reliable cheap and simple, but the downside was that they were smoky and incredibly inefficient. Despite this they became very popular in the farming and agricultural communities and Landini, realising he had fallen on a winning formula, decided to design his own hot bulb tractor.

Unfortunately, he died in 1924 so did not get to see his working prototype, model 25/30 of 1925. His sons took over the business, however, and carried on with the tractor project, producing the Super Landini model in the 1930s.

The Super Landini was used for land reclamation works in such places as the low-lying, waterlogged, malaria-infested Pontine Marshes.

With 48hp, the Super Landini was the most powerful tractor in Italy at that

PIONEERS AND INNOVATORS

time and stayed in production until the outbreak of World War II. Following the war, another powerful hot bulb tractor came out of the Landini factory: the L55, which stayed in production for 12 years.

Although the hot bulb engine was a success and these tractors are collector's items now, the Landini company realised that the future lay with diesel engines. In 1957, Landini signed a deal with Perkins Engines of Peterborough that permitted the production of British diesel engines in Italy. This led to the expansion of the Landini tractor range and in 1959, the company produced its first crawler tractor, Model C35. That same year, the Canadian firm of Massey-Ferguson took over Landini, giving the company financial security.

The years between the late 1960s and late 1980s marked a period of growth for the company. A new plant was opened in Aprilia specifically for the manufacture of earthmoving machines and in 1973 the product line was expanded to include the 7500, 6500 and 8500 with the revolutionary 12 + 4 gearbox.

Four years later, the original 'Large' series of tractors – the first European tractors of 100hp – was added to the range, and they were followed by a range of specialised tractors, notably for vineyards and orchards. Landini soon had 35 per cent of world sales of these specialist machines.

In 1994, Landini's ownership underwent another change when the Italians Valerio and Pierangelo Morra acquired majority shares in the company through the holding company of Argo, and they became president and vice-president respectively of Landini. Shortly after this, Landini acquired Valpadana, a prestigious name in small farm machinery.

In 1996, in order to meet growing demand, the company's Fabbrico manufacturing plant was dismantled and replaced by a new assembly line, designed to be capable of doubling production output. A new factory was also built at San Martino, just a few miles from the Fabbrico plant. These developments led to an agreement with the Japanese agricultural machine manufacturer Iseki for the provision of components and ultimately complete tractors – an agreement that continues to this day.

In the 2000s, new products have

continued to come out of Landini factories, including the Rex, Powerfarm, Alpine, Mistral America, Legend TDI, Starland, Powermaster, and Powermondial tractors. The latest series of tractors are the 5h and 7 Series, all of which are Tier 3-compliant. In 2011, the Landini Rex, a specialised tractor for orchard work, was crowned Tractor of the Year 2011 in the 'best of specialised' category at the Eima International trade fair in Bologna.

Massey-Ferguson

Massey-Ferguson grew out of the merger between Harry Ferguson's company and Massey-Harris in 1953, but the name wasn't coined until 1958. The name nowadays only exists as a brand name within the AGCO group.

Massey-Harris was founded in 1847 in Newcastle, Ontario, Canada, when Daniel Massey opened a workshop to build simple farm implements and the Newcastle Foundry and Machine Manufactory was formed. The firm was taken over and expanded by Daniel's eldest son, Hart Almerrin Massey, who renamed it the Massey Manufacturing Company. In 1879, he moved the company to Toronto, from where it became a worldwide success, selling internationally.

Meanwhile, in Ontario, Alanson Harris had established a foundry to make, repair and ultimately sell farm machinery. The two companies became arch-rivals as Harris sold the same kind of machinery as Massey. Both companies realised that a merger was inevitable for future success and in 1891 they got together to form the Massey-Harris Company.

Until the merger with Ferguson, the company sold under licence a variety of tractors, including the Minneapolis-built Bull. During the 1920s and 1930s they designed and built, with varying degrees of success, a range of their own tractors, the most innovative of which was the General Purpose, a three-speed, four-cylinder, 4WD machine with an articulated chassis. The plan was to lure farmers away from tracked tractors. This groundbreaking technology was way ahead of its time and in fact other manufacturers did not use it for another 20 to 30 years.

At the time of World War II, Massey-Harris began to update its entire fleet of tractors and, by the end of the war, they had brought out some entirely new models including the Pony, a small, lightweight, three-speed machine. This machine was assembled in France and became a success as it was well suited to the smaller fields of Europe and was available for some ten years.

In 1953, Massey-Harris merged with Harry Ferguson after his disagreement with Ford. This brought together two major producers with great skills in design and large factories in Canada,

LEFT
Massey-Ferguson Pony.
Credit Dual Freq

In 1994, the company was taken over by the AGCO group.

Currently, the largest agricultural tractor in the Massey Ferguson family is the 8690, a six-cylinder turbo cooled machine that was launched in Innovagri in France. This machine is the first in the world to feature SCR technology, which treats exhaust gases that would normally be released into the atmosphere using a special diesel exhaust fluid.

Minneapolis–Moline

Minneapolis–Moline was formed in 1929 by the merger of the Moline Implement Company, the Minneapolis Threshing Machine Company and the Minneapolis Steel and Machinery Company.

ABOVE The grille of a Twin City tractor. Credit Dual Freq

France, England and America capable of building vast numbers of machines. In addition, the combined enterprise had Ferguson's three-point hitch. This was a union that just could not fail.

To start with, the company produced separate lines of tractors as both manufacturers had loyal followers among their customers and dealers. At this time, the hyphen between the names was also dropped and the tractors were given red and grey livery.

In 1987, Massey Ferguson laid claim to being the largest tractor manufacturer in the western world, the 25th time it had achieved this feat.

The Minneapolis Steel and Machinery Company was the arm that was producing the Twin City range of tractors, and Minneapolis-Moline continued to produce this range until 1938. Initially, the Twin City brand name was kept but as the range evolved, so that name became less important and the Minneapolis-Moline name became more prominent. The first tractors

developed, produced and marketed under the Minneapolis-Moline brand name were called 'Visionlined'.

Minneapolis-Moline was a real innovator and the company pioneered a number of what were considered then to be new concepts. As we will see later on, in the chapter on oddities, they

developed the UDLX Comfortractor, with its steel cab and all manner of equipment normally only seen in a car.

Although this strange-looking vehicle was not a success, Minneapolis-Moline continued to build tractors and persevered with steel cabs in the form of the Model R and the ZTX. The Model

ABOVE Two Minneapolis-Moline tractors. Credit Dual Freq

R ran for a few years and was reasonably successful, but the ZTX was a complete failure with just 25 being built.

In 1963, Minneapolis-Moline was bought out by the White Motor Company, which had already purchased Oliver Farm Equipment in 1960 and Cockshutt Farm Equipment in 1962. White then started to sell all three makes of tractor under slightly different guises and in specific colour schemes depending on the brand. Thus Olivers were painted green, Cockshutts were red and Minneapolis-Molines were yellow but in essence they were exactly the same tractor.

In 1974, all tractors produced were brought under the White brand name and were painted in their own livery, naturally white. The White Tractor brand name disappeared entirely when the White Motor Company became part of the AGCO group in 1991.

New Holland

Mention in any book on tractors must be made of New Holland, yet New Holland itself never built any tractors, even though although it did build implements and, latterly, combine harvesters.

It all started in 1903, when Abe Zimmerman founded his company, New Holland Machine Company in – guess where? – New Holland, Pennsylvania. Prior to this, Zimmerman had been working on various agricultural products, mainly feed mills.

In 1947, the Sperry Corporation acquired the company, the name was changed to Sperry New Holland and production of feed mills, hay balers and combine harvesters continued. In 1964, Sperry New Holland purchased a major interest in Claeys, a big combine maker, and then in 1986 the whole lot was merged with Ford to form Ford New Holland.

Five years later, 80 per cent of the company was acquired by Fiat. A merger with Case followed, leading to the setting up of Case New Holland (CNH). Despite all these mergers, the New Holland name was kept on and tractors are still being badged under that name.

The latest New Holland concept is the NH2 hydrogen-powered tractor, the first such machine to be shown by any manufacturer. This tractor will be powered by hydrogen using electricity generated from photovoltaic panels, and

will produce no emissions other than a little water in the form of steam.

Oliver

The Oliver Chilled Plow Company was originally founded in 1855 by a Scottish immigrant to the USA called James Oliver. Oliver had patented a particularly hardened plough that was not only tough but could also work the thick, heavy soils of the American Midwest.

In the 1920s, Oliver began experimenting with tractors and in 1929 merged with The Hart-Parr Tractor Works, which was already established in the tractor business, Nichols and Shepard, a manufacturer of farm and mill machinery as well as steam engines, and the American Seeding Company, who were thriving in the seed drill business. The merger created the Oliver Farm Equipment Sales Company.

Soon after the merger, work began on developing a range of tractors that were based on Oliver's own designs; they were named model A & B row-crop prototypes. Though these machines were Oliver designs, they needed the Hart-Parr expertise to build them and initially they were called Oliver-Hart-Parr Row Crop. It was not long, though, before the Hart-Parr name was dropped.

This first model A had an adjustable rear axle which enabled the rear wheels to be adjusted according to the row spacing of the crop. Oliver was the first company to use adjustable wheels but, inevitably, other manufacturers were quick to latch on to the idea, and they soon followed suit. Tractors were available in Standard, Western, Ricefield and Orchard versions and were painted in a pale green with yellow trim around the grille and red wheels.

The next step forward that Oliver took was with the Model 70 Row Crop, which was introduced in 1935. Until then, most tractors had used low-compression, two- or four-cylinder engines running on either petrol or distillate; diesel had not yet come into production. The Oliver 70 was particularly streamlined compared to other, far boxier tractors, and it was fitted with a high-compression, six-cylinder engine. In addition, an electric starter and lights were optional extras. It truly was groundbreaking.

Over the following ten years, Oliver brought out a range of tractors, some slightly more powerful than the 70 and some slightly less, but they were all more or less rebadged versions of previous models. It was not until 1948 and the introduction of the Fleetline range of 66, 77 and 88 tractors that Oliver brought out some restyling. The 88 was available in a range of petrol, diesel and paraffin engines. In addition, parts were interchangeable among the Fleetline models.

The Super series 88 & 99 followed during the 1950s, and they carried a lighter green and white paint scheme.

The 99 was the biggest tractor of its day, sold well in excess of expectation and stayed in production for 20 years.

In 1960, Oliver was bought by the White Motor Corporation along with, a short while later, Minneapolis-Moline and Cockshutt. The Oliver name continued throughout the 1960s and into the 1970s, although sometimes virtually the same tractor was badged as an Oliver and also a Minneapolis-Moline. For example, the Oliver model 2655 was the same as the Minneapolis-Moline A4T-1600, or the Oliver model 2455 which was the same as the Minneapolis-Moline A4T-1400. The only difference was the paint colour. As we saw before, Oliver were painted green and Minneapolis-Moline were yellow.

In 1973, the name Oliver was dropped and in 1985, the Oliver Chilled Plow works were closed down. The company was absorbed into AGCO in 1990.

Steiger

Steiger, which is now part of the Case group, has its origins in the America of the 1950s. Brothers Douglas and Maurice Steiger, who farmed around

4,000 acres in Minnesota, had specific needs for their land and required a big, powerful tractor.

At that time they couldn't find anything suitable on the market, so they decided to design their own tractor. They built a massive 4WD tractor in one of their barns and called it Steiger No 1.

From that early tractor, Steiger gained a reputation for building massive machines. They went on to build a total

of 120 tractors, all assembled in that original barn and all named after big cats – Puma, Bearcat, Cougar, Panther, Lion and Tiger – with each name relating to a specific horsepower class. In order to be different from other tractor manufacturers, they also chose a distinctive lime green livery.

In 1969, Steiger lost their autonomy when they were incorporated into a large business consortium and moved to Fargo in North Dakota. The Steiger name was continued even though they were building tractors for other companies; mainly Allis-Chalmers and Ford. When Case bought out the company in 1986, they continued to keep the Steiger name as it was a byword for well-built, powerful, 4WD machines.

Steiger tractors are now painted in Case colours but they still carry the reputation for being probably the best 4WD tractors in the world.

Valtra

Valtra is another tractor model that is rarely seen in Britain, yet it is the fourth largest tractor manufacturer in the world.

Valtra is a Scandinavian company that can trace its roots right back to 1832, when Johan Theofron Munktell founded the Eskilstuna Mekaniska Werkstad in what is considered to be the beginning of the industrial history of both Valtra and Volvo.

Munktell began by manufacturing steam and traction engines, but in 1913 he built his first agricultural tractor. This model, the Munktell 30-40, was huge and very heavy, so three years later, the company introduced a lighter model. With the success of this tractor, Munktell stopped building traction engines and started to concentrate on tractors.

Little happened during the war years but in 1950 Munktell was acquired by Volvo and a year later, the Valmet 15 was built. By the spring of 1955, 3,000 of these tractors had been sold but Finnish farmers wanted something more powerful, so the Valmet 20 was introduced. Both the Valmet 15 and Valmet 20 had 1.5 litre engines; the Valmet 15 had just 15hp whereas the Valmet 20 power was 19.5-22hp and it weighed some 120kg more. By 1956, Valmet had branched out into diesel-engined tractors.

Probably the best-loved of all Valtra models was the BM Volvo T 350 Boxer

,with its innovative transmission: ten forward gears and two reverse. In 1964 a synchromesh gearbox was fitted to the 40hp Valmet 565; a synchro tractor was a totally new innovation. The advertisements for this tractor put it succinctly: "Now you drive your tractor like your car".

Another Valtra innovation was introduced just three years later: the integrated safety cab, a feature that we regard as the norm nowadays.

In 1969, Valtra made history again when the model 1100, "stronger than strong", was introduced. As far as was known, the 1100 was the first tractor in the world with a turbocharged four-cylinder 4.2 litre, 115hp diesel engine. It was also equipped with eight forward and two reverse gears and four-wheel drive.

In 1971, the company launched a mid range of tractors. This was the Valmet 502, claimed to have the quietest cab in the world. The noise level was officially measured at N 85, which meant the tractor operator could work in the cab for up to five hours without any detrimental effect on his or her hearing.

Another innovation for which the company was responsible was the colour scheme of the tractor. Originally, all Valtra tractors were painted red, but this was changed in 1968 to yellow and then, in 1982, back to red. Later in the 1980s, Valtra introduced five other colours for their tractors, the intention being that the customer could choose his or her own option.

Nowadays, all Valtra tractors are made to order and individually built to meet the specific needs of the customer via the Valtra A la Carte system. Valtra also give their customers the opportunity to see their tractor being built in the factory.

In 1994, Valmet was acquired by Sisu, a Finnish truck company and an agreement was made whereby the Valmet name would be phased out by April 2001. Initially the tractors were renamed Valtra Valmet, but then Valmet was wholly dropped. In January 2004, AGCO acquired the tractor business and, with the support of this concern, Valtra has become the second most popular brand of tractors in Latin America and the market leader in China in the over-120hp class.

A Medley
Of Oddities

Until now, the focus has been on standard farm tractors of differing size and power. But there are a number of companies that specialise in giant tractors, generally aimed at the North American prairie and Canadian wheat farmer.

The biggest tractor in existence today is Big Bud 747, which was built in Havre, Montana in 1977 by Ron Harmon and the crew of the Northern Manufacturing Company at a cost then of $300,000. Big Bud 747, one of just 600 Big Bud brand tractors ever built, was designed to the specifications of the Rossi Brothers, who were cotton farmers in California.

This giant tractor is fitted with a 24.1 litre Detroit Diesel V16 92 turbo engine that produces around 760hp but has the potential of reaching 1100hp. The tyres are a massive 2.3 metres tall and they were made especially by the United Tyre Company of Canada. The fuel tank holds 1,000 US gallons and there is a 150 gallon hydraulic reservoir for the steering and implement control system. When the fuel tank is full, the tractor weighs in at around 46,000kg.

Big Bud measures an enormous 8.2 metres long, 6 metres wide and 4.3 metres tall, and has a 4.8 metre wheelbase. It has six forward gears and one reverse that drive all the wheels. The tractor works at the impressive rate of one acre per minute, ploughing to a depth of a metre while travelling at 8 mph.

The Rossi Brothers used the tractor for 11 years before it was sold to Willowbrook Farms in Florida, where it was again used for deep ploughing. Put into retirement in 1997, it was bought by the Williams Brothers of Montana, who took it to their farm in Chouteau

County. The Williams brothers upgraded the engine from the original 760hp to 900hp and used the tractor for cultivation purposes, pulling an 80-foot cultivator. They also gave it a new paint job and chrome exhaust stacks.

Big Bud was finally put into retirement by the Williams brothers and placed on display at the Heartland Acres Agribition Centre in Iowa, where it remains to this day. The Northern Manufacturing Company built a range of behemoths, but they went bankrupt in the early 1980s and were bought up by the Messner Brothers. They carried on producing tractors but, owing to a recession in farming and competition from other manufacturers, the last Big Bud came off the production line in 1992.

Several other manufacturers now offer enormous tractors. Among the names that immediately spring to mind are Fendt, JCB, Steiger and ACO 2000. Four-wheel drive has been the norm for large tractors since the 1970s, but Fendt brought out a six-wheel drive concept tractor in 2007, calling it the Trisix.

Although it might not be the first six-wheeled tractor ever, it will certainly be the most powerful one by far. If the Trisix goes into production it will have a reputed 540hp rating. The MAN 12.4 litre engine will be powered by rapeseed oil and the machine will have a top speed of over 40mph. It is envisaged that the Trisix will be capable of being driven legally on motorways.

The planned overall length is 7.6 metres and the width 2.75 metres. The Trisix will have three axles and will be fitted with six wheels, each a metre high. To ensure that all the power is transmitted to the ground and to avoid the soil becoming compacted, there will be a tyre pressure control system which is under patent. The front axle will be mechanically steered while electronics will communicate information between the two transmissions that power the mid and rear axles.

There are plans to allow the mid axle to extend, thus allowing the tyres to travel on fresh ground. All six wheels will have independent hydraulic suspension that can be lowered to pick equipment. The planned turning circle will be just 14.4 metres – quite an achievement for such a large machine.

At present there are almost 30 patents

LEFT
The 1955
Trans Antarctic
Expedition
Tractor on
display in the
Canterbury
Museum

A MEDLEY OF ODDITIES

for the Trisix, and these include the high performance brakes, special fuel tanks located on the rear wheels, the complete exhaust manifold and a brand new forced air engine cooling system.

Porsche, a name synonymous with upmarket sports cars, made a venture into the field of tractors between 1934 and the early 1960s. Most of their designs were nothing out of the ordinary, but they did produce around 300 bright orange tractors to be used on Brazilian coffee plantations.

The Coffee Train P312 looks somewhat like two dodgem cars sitting atop one another with a steering wheel under cover and enclosed wheels. It was built to be streamlined so that it wouldn't snag on the coffee plants. The P312 was built to run on petrol as the plantation owners didn't want diesel fumes near their valuable crops.

The Ferguson TE20 was one of the most successful of all of the Ferguson tractors and, during the period between 1955 and 1958, three were modified to be used to ferry supplies and people during the Trans Antarctic Expeditions by Sir Edmund Hillary. The main modifications to

the standard TE20 were an extra axle with track conversion and a Duncan canvas cover for the cab and engine. Most of the tractors were left at the South Pole for future expeditions, but the one in the picture on page 89 was taken to Christchurch, New Zealand.

Another oddity for our list is the distinctively named Bates Steel Mule tractor. No one could accuse this heavy tractor of being pretty. With normal steel tractor wheels at the front that did the steering, tank-type treads on the rear, a long steering column and the driver seat set far back, almost off the end of the tractor, it really was quite a distinctive spectacle when in action.

Another unusual monster was the GMC Samson three-wheeled Sieve Grip tractor, whose name comes from its huge open steel wheels with cleats. The manufacturers alleged that the open treads provided better traction.

The body of the tractor is so long that the driver cannot actually see where he is going. To compensate for this drawback, a large arrow had to be fitted directly over the front wheel to give the driver some indication as to his direction. Fortunately, the machine's top

A MEDLEY OF ODDITIES

speed was a little over 3mph. Another peculiarity was the water-filled air cleaner that had the wonderful name of Nodust Moisto Rizer.

Another odd three-wheeler tractor was the Wallace Glasgow, which was built just after World War I. This tractor had three equal-sized steel wheels, all of which were driven, and so it became reasonably popular in hilly country and where the ground was waterlogged. The Glasgow had a system of ratchets that were fitted to the two front wheels instead of a differential. This ensured that the two front wheels had the maximum grip while turning at the correct speed.

How about crossing the sea in a caterpillar tractor ferry? In 1935 just such a vehicle was seen plying the seas around the British coast, and similar types of vehicle are still in existence today. Carrying passengers high up in an open trailer, these precarious, top heavy tractors are not for the faint-hearted. The particular tractor in the picture is the only one of its kind in the world. It was designed in 1969 by Robert Jackson CBE, allegedly in exchange for a case of champagne!

From the sea, we now go to the air

and aircraft tow tractors. Again, these don't look anything like conventional tractors in the usual sense of the word. There are two types of tow tractors – pushback ones and tow bar-less ones – and they are both designed to move commercial aircraft whether they are empty or fully laden.

One experiment that failed was the Minneapolis-Moline UDLX (Ultra deluxe), otherwise known as the Comfortractor. Just around 125 of these odd-looking yet futuristic machines were built, yet when they were introduced in 1938 they were designed to be the answer to every farmer's problems. The farmer could work in the field with his UDLX during the week and then drive in it to the town at weekends – it was a cross between a car and a tractor.

It had a fully enclosed, heated cab with passenger seat, windows that could open, a cigarette lighter and glove box, even headlights – the standard set up of a car. The top speed on the roads was 45mph – perhaps a bit slow, but then was it a tractor or was it a car?

LEFT The odd looking Minneapolis-Moline UDLX. Credit Trekphiler

LEFT A tow bar less tractor at Schipol Airport, Amsterdam. Credit Barcex

Tractor
Pulling

RIGHT
Preparing the track.

The sport of tractor pulling did not reach Great Britain until the mid 1970s, but it had been a sport in America from the late 19th century when farmers would organise competitions to find the best team of pulling horses.

In the 1920s, once farmers had started to use tractors instead of horses, the sport was adapted for these machines. It would appear that the first official tractor pulling events took place in 1929 at Bowling Green, Missouri and Vaughansville, Ohio, but the sport did not become truly popular until the 1960s.

The sport consists of a trailer or sledge with weights on it, which is attached to a tractor by means of a chain. The rules are slightly more complicated, but the basic principle is simple: the winner is the tractor that can pull the trailer the furthest. The sledge can come in all manner of shapes and sizes, sometimes with wheels and sometimes without.

Originally just a standard farm tractor was used but now all kinds of modifications are allowed, and the

tractors compete in a complex array of classes. Eventually, the tractors lost their farming appearance and began to look like dragsters. This led to all kinds of stock classes being created so that everyone could compete – Super-Stock,

Pro-Stock and mini-modified.

The first tractor pulling events in Europe took place in 1977 and the British Tractor Pullers Association (BTPA) was formed in 1978. Competition in Britain takes place on a

100 metre long track. If a driver completes the entire 100 metres, it is called a full pull. If more than one machine completes the 100 metres, then the trailer or sledge is made harder to pull.

In Britain the classes consist of Super Farm class, in which a standard farm tractor limited to one turbocharger and a RPM limit of 2800 is used; Under 401 Pro-Stock class, which also uses a standard machine but now with no RPM limit; the Pro-Stock class, which again is limited to one turbocharger but larger engines up to 8.36 litres; and the Super-Stock class. The last is the class for the most highly tuned machines.

Most engines are diesel-powered but some competitors use methane. All the above classes compete at 3.5 tons, which is the weight of the machine and driver added together. Within the modified classes, practically any engine modification is acceptable, and this is when the tractors start to look like dragsters.

There are tractor pulling associations in England, Ireland, Scotland and Wales, but tractor pulling is also a popular sport throughout Australia and Europe – especially the Scandinavian countries, Germany, France and Russia.

LEFT Tractor Pulling. Credit Dirk Ingo Franke

Museums
And Collections

There are a number of museums dotted around Britain with very interesting collections of tractors – and most of these collections contain vintage models.

Let us start in the south of the country and work northwards. The Ferguson Family Museum at Freshwater on the Isle of Wight was opened in 2003 by the grandson of tractor man Harry Ferguson. The museum details the story of Harry's life, from his humble upbringing to his success as one of the greatest tractor pioneers of all time. Although the museum is not open to the general public, it can be opened by appointment. It contains many artefacts relating to Ferguson's work, including the Brown Tractor.

The Coldridge Collection in mid-Devon has a fine selection of Ferguson tractors, including a Ferguson Brown from 1936, a 1943 Ford Ferguson 9N, a couple of restored 1947 TE20s and TED20s, a couple of TEF20s; from the 1950s a selection of MF35s, MF65s, MF135s and an MF1020. In addition, it has a vast collection of implements and accessories related to Ferguson tractors. This is another private collection but can be opened on request.

The Science Museum in London also has an example of a Harry Ferguson tractor. In the collection is an original Black Tractor from the 1930s.

The excellent Oakham Treasures is an impressive privately owned museum near Portbury, Bristol. It has a section devoted entirely to tractors and farming implements and, in fact, houses around 150 old and vintage machines, most still in working order with the oldest example being a 1918 Fordson.

Not all that far from Oakham

Treasures can be found the Lackham Museum of Agricultural and Rural Life, near Chippenham in Wiltshire. Here on display is a Waterloo Boy tractor. It seems likely that this particular model was imported in dismantled form and then restored to full working order by the Overtime Tractor Company.

Toddington Manor in Bedfordshire houses Sir Neville Bowman-Shaw's tractor collection. This is another exciting collection, with an Allis-Chalmers Model B, a 1911 Case, a Fordson F and a 1959 John Deere 730. In total there are around 50 models in the collection.

Also in Bedfordshire is the privately owned Stondon Museum, which has a small but impressive display of tractors. Over the border in Cambridgeshire is the Farmland Museum and Denny Abbey. This collection focuses on farming in the region and there are three tractors on display: a grey Fergie, a Fordson N and a Farmall.

The Yorkshire Museum of Farming, located just outside York, opened in 1982 and has a large and diverse collection of tractors as well as ploughs,

binders and reapers. There are plans to have a house devoted entirely to Ferguson tractors and paraphernalia.

The Ryedale Folk museum is another collection located in Yorkshire, and it has a selection of tractors on display. In addition, each year the museum holds a tractor day and exhibitors from all over the country come to show their prized machines.

In Scotland, one of the best places to see tractors and agricultural implements is the National Museum of Rural Life in East Kilbride. Various Ferguson, Ford Ferguson and International Harvester tractors are on display.

LEFT
A Fordson Super Major with trailer.
Credit Bangin

Security

RIGHT
High-Tech
interior of a
modern John
Deere tractor

A great concern for the tractor owner of today and tomorrow is security. With some new tractors costing upwards of £100,000 in Britain, it's surprising that many are not fitted with supplementary security devices.

If the truth be told, security on farming equipment is incredibly lax. Quite often a standard ignition key will fit many vehicles, making them easy targets for thieves. In fact, £36 million worth of tractors and digger equipment is stolen and resold in the UK every year; usually the items are stolen to order and transported quickly out of the country to eastern Europe, Africa or the Middle East.

But in addition to immobilisers, there are a variety of hidden and open security systems available to farmers, and one of the invisible systems is data dots.

These consist of minute dots, about the size of a grain of sand, on to which is laser-etched a unique identification number or code. The dots can be stuck to any surface and it is virtually impossible to locate or remove them. The code relates to the individual tractor and if the machine is stolen and then recovered, it is a simple task to track down the owner.

DNA security marking system is a glue-based system. The DNA comes in a pot of glue that is applied to the tractor. Each pot contains at least 1,000 microdots, allowing for practically total uniqueness. The dots are invisible and also impossible to remove. Once the DNA glue has been applied, the information is transferred to a database and should the item be stolen, it is then an easy process for the stolen goods to be returned to their rightful owner.

Another hidden system consists of a small glass transponder about the size of a grain of rice that contains a unique code number which is permanently programmed with the owner's information. These can be fitted anywhere on a tractor. The transponders have neither moving parts nor a battery, so they should last for ever. This makes them perfect for outdoor environments.

A device reads the transponder information; communication is accomplished using radio frequency signals and so they are an excellent tracking device. Transponders are difficult to counterfeit and the information held within them cannot be altered or deleted.

The unique identification plate works in a similar way. Information is etched on to a triangular plate that is fitted on to the tractor. These plates are tamper-proof and carry a unique number ensuring that the property can be tracked and traced. Again, the information on the plates is very difficult to alter and almost impossible to remove.

All John Deere, Landini and McCormick tractors have been fitted with four of these plates somewhere on the body or chassis since 2010.

The Future

As we saw earlier, the future for tractors would seem to lie in hydrogen-powered machines, but what would these machines actually look like?

Styling is an important issue for tractor manufacturers and for a company to be successful nowadays, it is necessary for their machines not just to function well, be economical to run and comply with the latest emissions laws but also to look good.

Naturally, most manufacturers want all of their machines to come out of the same stable so that they look similar, not just on the outside but also internally. And the trend for the last ten years or so has been to make tractors less boxy and more rounded with sleek curves.

One of the major issues affecting how future tractors will look in the future involves their power source; if it is to be hydrogen, there will need to be space under the bonnet for the fuel cells. But whatever method is chosen, all the major manufacturers are at present investing huge sums of money in research and development.

One machine that is already in production but hasn't yet reached these shores is the Challenger MT975, the largest and most powerful tractor ever built. With its six-cylinder 18.1 litre engine and a tank capacity of fuel 1,500 litres (390 gallons), this monster of a machine would take 20 minutes for a complete fill. At 509cm or 200 inches wide and 756 cm or 298 inches long, would this behemoth fit in our fields, never mind our roads?

One concept still on the drawing board that could come to see the light of day is the Case New Holland CNH XTE 9: a blend of tractor and motor car, a concept that was tried out years ago by Minneapolis–Moline with their none too successful UDLX Comfortractor. Could things be different in the modern era, and would the farmer of tomorrow want a vehicle that could be used in the field and also as a family car?

Case is also in the process of developing a 1,000hp tractor, the Case IH Quadtrac. The concept was originally shown to the world over ten years ago, and it will be interesting to

see if it ever goes into production.

Another Case tractor still in the planning stages is the Magnum 250, for which work is being carried out in the Netherlands. It is planned for the Magnum 250 to be kitted out with rubber tracks on all four corners, which will amount to more than 7 metres of rubber being used in total. The total weight of the tractor, including the four track units, will be 14.8 tons and the machine will be fitted with standard 76cm wide tracks at the rear while at the front, specially designed 61cm wide units will need to be developed.

Many of these concepts are shrouded in mystery. It has been reported that Case IH has a Puma tractor which allegedly runs on liquefied petroleum gas (LPG), but if they have, they are keeping it very much a secret.

Valtra is a Scandinavian company

that is working on several new products, some of which are not planned for release until 2020. In its future line-up it has the Valtra N101, which it plans to run on biogas, produced from chicken litter and pig slurry, using a conventional diesel engine block. On the model that is being tested in Sweden, the biogas cylinders are situated on the right side of the chassis and their capacity is 170 litres, which corresponds to around 30 litres of diesel or three to four hours of work.

Advances made on the navigation front are paving the way for driverless tractors, which could dispense altogether with a cab, although current legislation prevents this. Valtra's RoboTrac would be one such vehicle. It has been designed to perform a range of tasks such as ploughing, planting or spraying through a pre-programmed, driverless system. GPS and the internet would be used to track its location. The RoboTrac would also feature a 85hp diesel engine and rear wheel steering in either two-wheel or four-wheel drive configurations.

John Deere is also looking into the possibility of an autonomous tractor. Instructions would be given to the tractor via a computerised route plan and the theory is that the tractor will be able to follow the route automatically, regardless of any obstacles in its way. But the fear is that today's sensing technologies aren't reliable enough to ensure an autonomous tractor will stop should an emergency arise.

Another tractor not yet available to British farmers is the limited edition Valtra Revolution, as at present they are only available in Finland and are a limited edition of just 50. These tractors are based on the Advance models T141, T171 and N191, but they are painted in a black metallic livery. Standard features include cab suspension, xenon work lights, air-suspended front axle, electrically operated and heated mirrors and a specially-developed steering wheel complete with temperature control.

The Italian designer Victor Uribe has been developing the Unimog (a German acronym for universal-motor-gerät) tractor for Mercedes Benz. This machine is still in the concept stage, but the design is based around the cabin of a jet fighter. Uribe has planned the tractor to have multiple uses, from towing aircraft to a simple transporter.

Made of carbon fibre, basalt fibre and aluminium and thus very light, it features infrared sensors on the front to convey to the driver signals about the driving surface as well as solar panels on the roof. The concept vehicle has six wheels, each of which contains powerful electric motors that keep the driving noise down to an absolute minimum – especially useful when used in an urban environment.

In addition to new designs, manufacturers and others are working on ensuring new tractors that come off the production line will be interim Tier 4- and, ultimately, entirely Tier 4-compliant. Interim Tier 4, which takes effect in 2011, requires diesel engines with 174hp or more to reduce particulate matter emissions by 90 per cent, and nitrogen oxide emissions by 50 per cent.

The full Tier 4 regulations will take particulate matter and nitrogen oxide emissions to near-zero levels by 2015. All the major manufacturers are working hard on their engines to find a solution to cutting emissions, and many of them are working on similar yet different principles.

To download our latest catalogue and to view
the full range of books and DVDs visit:

www.G2ent.co.uk

ALSO AVAILABLE IN THE LITTLE BOOK SERIES

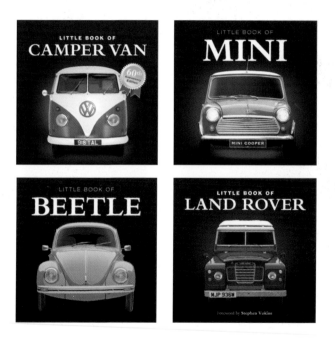

The pictures in this book were provided courtesy of the following:

JOHN DEERE
www.deere.com

SHUTTERSTOCK
www.shutterstock.com

Design and artwork by Scott Giarnese

Published by G2 Entertainment Limited

Publishers Jules Gammond and Edward Adams

Written by Ellie Charleston